Billion $ Blueprint
WORKSHOP WORKBOOK
Hal Barr | 4/1/2016

Selling

INTRODUCTION

The purpose of this workshop workbook is to reinforce the information shared in the book "THE FIRST BILLION'$ THE TOUGHEST". The system that is talked extensively about in the book has a proven track record and has been employed by some of the best professional sales people in the country. The practice management tools described in this workbook are practical and impactful and have shown measurable and immediate results. For any sales professional looking to improve his or her game and prosper in their practice, this straight forward workbook will provide the insights and the tools to accomplish your greatest desires.

Not only have the principles talked about in this workbook help you on a professional level but many individuals say it has helped them in their personal lives as well. What people who are successful need is balance in their lives, which unless you do the occasional gut check, you can easily lose a proper prospective on life. Take the time to do the exercises in this book and it will no doubt help you in ways you would not thought possible.

Why should I listen to Hal Barr?

Nationally recognized thought leader on business development. Hal presented the 80/20 Principles over 180 times a year for the past 5 years to Fortune 100 companies. With over 30 years of in the trenches personal sales experience, Hal strategies have helped thousands of independent business people in the US grow top line revenue from 25% to 125%.

Personal sales highlights....

- Made over $4 billion in sales over his career in both products and services
- Raising $100 million in 60 days on new product introduction for a major US asset management firm
- Opening a new a territory with 0 sales growing to $30 million in one year
- Increasing asset growth from $250 million per year to $2 billion over the next three years for a major $800 billion international asset manager
- Reviving sales in an undeveloped territory for one of the largest insurance companies in the US from $3 million to $30 million to $50 million to $100 million in three years

Sales is possibly the hardest profession in the world because professionals are tainted by those that don't do it right. This book is your guide to how to improve your skills to be the professional that others will admire and emulate. The methods discussed in this book have been tested and worked for literally thousands of sales people throughout the US and beyond. -Learn to Speak the way people are willing to listen -Understand who your clients are that truly deserve your time and attention -Streamline your business and become more successful with less stress Hal Barr has over 30 years in sales during which he developed and authored a proven sales process that increases sales, revenues and client retention. The process is based on the Pareto Principle which is almost considered a law of nature.

"Let me be totally honest with you; I'm writing the book I wish someone had given me when I first started in the sales game," explains Barr. "I made a huge number of mistakes, was forced to learn through trial-and-error and I'm now taking readers beyond that point, so they don't have to attend the same sales school of hard knocks. Over the years I've developed a very strategic and proven methodology that has become the "80/20" principles. This book marks the first time I've made them available to the general public without charging tens of thousands in consulting fees."

- Continuing, "I suggest that anyone planning to make sales their long-term profession should read it now and reread it every year. It's vital to always remain grounded to the foundations, and each time professionals read the book they'll see information in a fresh new context and have creative new ways to deploy it to their advantage." Since its release, critics have come out in force with rave reviews. For example, Doug Ikenberry comments, "This is a book that can make you money. It jumps way past the "theory of selling" and shows a budding sales professional HOW to do it. It starts with explaining the art of selling to different types of people and moves into the science of how to approach a book of business to maximize production. It ends with real world advice on managing your career as you advance in your field."

- M. Liberato adds, "Hal has concisely written a "must read" for sales professionals! His anecdotal experience and philosophical viewpoints hit the mark on the very dynamic world of professional sales. His extensive focus on the business-to-business approach to sales is an invaluable goldmine for anyone looking to sharpen their overall sales approach and techniques. I highly recommend "The First Billion$ The Toughest" I have been in professional sales for 35 years, I thoroughly enjoyed Hals book and am buying one for my son who is graduating college and about to enter the professional world of selling!"

Testimonials

Sanford Simmons   *RVP at Behringer Securities*
Hal's high energy and positive outlook coupled with his world class speaking skills were a tremendous resource for me when tasked with sharing investment concepts with financial advisors. His great sense of humor adds to his proficiency as a great communicator.

Mark McMeans   *CEO, Brasada Capital Management*
Hal is one of those people that you'd rather not have to speak after in a program since he's one of the best public speakers that you'll see. He's a great communicator, a real pro at his job and I enjoyed working with him so many years at AIM.

Alan Gray   *Vice President at Wellesley Investment Advisors, Inc.*
Hal is one of the best presenters I have worked with. He has a way of taking complicated subjects and making them simple to understand. He was always well received at conferences we worked together and was a sought after speaker. Hal was a pleasure to work with

Jim Webb   *Chairman at J.P. Webb Advisory*
Hal is above all, a professional. He is bonafide resource for insight regarding trends in

a broad array of sales & marketing disciplines and equally adept in providing leadership regarding the "best practices" for individuals & groups to pursue and maximize their greatest benefits from correctly anticipating and adjusting to these changing landscapes. His decades of experience within all phases of the financial services industry makes him a key advisor in this marketplace. I would not hesitate to recommend Hal to any organization.

Bob Sergent, CSP *Regional Sales Manager/ Product Manager at Containment Solutions*
I consider it a privilege to know Hal. I know other people that share the same sentiments. Hal is a pleasure to work with. His communication style and demeanor around people is inviting. His trust for maintaining confidentiality is beyond reproach. I am proud to be associated with this individual.

Jeff Heard CFP®, CIMA® *Director; Financial Advisor at UBS Wealth Management*
I've known Hal almost 8 years, and have always been impressed with his professionalism, integrity, and attention to detail. When communicating (whether with Advisors or Clients), he is able to take a complex message and translate it into a simple story that Clients can connect with.

Terri Fiedler *Executive Vice President, Strategic Accounts at AIG Financial Distributors*
Hal's strong speaking skills led him to take a position as a full-time presenter helping financial advisors grow their business. Hal was one of our most sought after presenters and delivered creative and impactful presentations.

Billion $ Blueprint

Now the fun begins…..

The first thing we are going to look at is what is it that motivates you and to that end you need to answer the following questions truthfully and in heartfelt conviction. No answers are right or wrong and none of the answers will reflect badly upon you as an individual, they are merely away to assess what it is that will get you focused and moving to the next level in your practice.

Let's start with the basics……

What are you most motivated by?

Money

Family

Free time/ Travel/ Hobbies

Recognition/Advancement

What is your current business like?

Successful

Moderate

Needs Help

Crisis

What obstacles are keeping you from taking it to the next level?

Money

Time

Expertise

Organization / Support

Clients

What are the major passions in your life?

Family

Travel

Hobbies

Serving others

Other

Do you think you are coachable, can take advice and employ action without accountability?

Yes

No

Do you know what your time is worth? Is it your gross income divided by 52 weeks divided by 40 hours?

Think very carefully about your answer, the answer may seem easy, but I will share with you another way to think about your time and what it is truly worth.

Next task to see if you are ready is to take out a calendar and complete the following assignment.

Mark down on the calendar your basic needs and obligations. Things to consider: holidays, birthdays, anniversaries, family vacations, personal time, significant other time, community service, missions, business required meetings, major events such as graduations and weddings. If you are married block of 4 weekends away with your spouse and that means that two of the weekends you are responsible for making plans and the other two your spouse is to make the plans. Whatever the plans are the other has to go along and experience and enjoy the time together.

Why are these first two exercises important?

If we don't know what our time is worth we may be doing things which others could do for us a lot cheaper, quicker and with better results. It is important to know how much value there is in our chosen profession or else we might be likely to squander our time on things that are not as important as making profitable use of our time. There are times to delegate some responsibilities which need to be done but do not add at all to our productivity.

List some of the things which you do that someone else could do cheaper and with more productivity and expertise than you and would free you up to enjoy your time more?

1.
2.
3.
4.
5.
6.

Selling

Life can be so complicated and to try to balance all the things that we are responsible for is a never ending list. If we don't take control of our time and life someone or something else will. That is why we need to really set our priorities straight and make certain we control them and not allow them to control us. I have heard it said that very successful people when they reach their final days don't wish they could make one more sale or be in one more meeting, they wish they had spent more time doing the things with the people they loved and doing the things that made them happy. Some of these same people are the ones that brag about how many hours they work and all the vacation time they are owed or have never taken. That is just pathetic. These people have no idea what they are missing in their lives and they are going to end up having a bucket list without a single item checked off. Sad, very sad.

Selling 80

THE ART OF THE SALE

As we go through our sales career we are constantly trained on the product and services which we provide. We are taught about the consultative sale, the problem solver approach, the FAB method, the pain relief method but the one area that most professionals are lacking is understanding the obligation we have to speak to people in a manner in which they are prepared to listen. Very often we are so excited about the fact we are getting to speak with someone we can't wait to jump into the pitch and show them how much we know and how sure we know the product or service can be their solution.

Some people have a certain knack for getting people to trust them and want to do business with them. These people are a rare breed or they have been taught one of the most important things in sales and the is

Talking to people the way they are prepared to listen.

This is a skill set that most people even if they are successful are totally unaware of. They have just got the ability to emulate the people they are dealing with and understand almost intuitively what they are willing to do and how to satisfy their need. They ingratiate themselves to these people in a way that is natural and unimposing.

But what is it that they understand consciously or subconsciously that most people don't? Most of you have been subject to a test of your personality type at one time or another in your career whether it was a Myers Briggs, DISC or any number of personality profiling. Companies rely on these tools to place people in certain positions depending on their natural disposition and EQ. If you want to be an outstanding sales professional you must understand a person's natural demeanor and apply some psychology to your conversation.

So what do you and should you know about people?

Let's start with the basics. What are the categories people fall into? Rather than name off some of the previous descriptors of these personalities I have developed my own vernacular. They are as follows:

The **THINKER** needs to be **Right**   15%-20%

- Always start with providing information
- Give the THINKER time to think through the information and be prepared to answer their questions
- Make certain every situation starts with any questions, then provide follow up on unanswered questions or provide data
- These individuals suffer from analysis paralysis and need to be comfortable to make a decision
- NEVER START SELLING TILL THEY HAVE FULLY VETTED THE INFORMATION

The **TASKER** needs to be **Appreciated**   35%-40%

- These are the worker bees
- They want to know what needs to be done and the importance of that work
- They want to be part of the discussion but don't want to be singled out for their thoughts
- They want to be acknowledged in different ways according to their personalities, it could be words, gifts, acknowledge in front of people
- RARELY SHOW INITIATIVE BUT ARE AWESOME AT COMPLETING THE TASK

The **TELLER** needs to be in **Control**   15%-20%

- Be brief and to the point
- No time for niceties yet, personal questions make people uncomfortable
- Have clear understanding of the facts and NEVER answer with what you think they want to hear, future revisions makes them skeptical
- Pay attention to the gate keepers but not too familiar till you are invited to go there
- BE TRANSPARENT AND NEVER LET A TELLER GET BAD NEWS FROM ANY ONE BUT YOU

The **TALKER** needs to be **Liked**   25%-30%

- These people want to have a rapport with you before they will do business
- Be personable and friendly
- Ask lots of questions about them
- Once you connect with them they will bring up business
- They usually in the know about what is going on in the office
- They are anxious to introduce you to others because they tend to be relationship junkies
- DON'T LET THEM OVERLOOK THAT YOU

There is another way to tell what type of EQ space someone occupies. The Thinkers and Tellers are more logical whereas the Talkers and Taskers are more emotional. The Thinkers and the Taskers tend to be more introverted where the Tellers and theTalkers tend to be more extroverted.

	Teller	**Talker**	**Tasker**	**Thinker**
Talking	Gets to the point	Tells stories	No opinions	Precise
Listening	Poor listener	Doesn't hear details	Sympathetic listener	Seeks facts
Handshake	Firm	Enthusiastic	Gentile	Brief
Personal Space	Maintains distance	Likes to be close	Tactile	Avoids Contact
Movement	Bold	Quick	Slow	Controlled
Workspace	Suggests power	Cluttered	Displays phots	Organized

EXERCISE

Make a list of ten people you talk or relate to on a daily basis. The first five individuals should be on the personal side of life like your spouse, children, siblings, parents and so on. The second five should be those people that you have to deal with daily at work, and these should include coworkers, clients, bosses, the public or the server at your favorite restaurant. Ensure that, at least, one from each list is a person that often proves him/her difficult to deal

with. This is because we want to try a new approach with them based on what we have learned so far. Bear in mind that when you talk to people the way they are willing to listen, the results can be immediate and astounding. Try to identify their particular style of communication, remind yourself how they are willing to listen and adjust your delivery accordingly. Practice this regularly and keep the chart of personalities with you to review whenever you are meeting with someone for the first time or find yourself in a frustrating communication.

Personal Relationships

1.
2.
3.
4.
5.

Business Relationships

1.
2.
3.
4.
5.

Now think about the way you have been speaking to them. Are you talking to these people in a manner in which they are able to listen? This revelation may make your communications easier and much more fruitful. I have had any number of people when they realize what it is about the person they are trying to communicate with and how they have been trying to do it in the past, it becomes very clear as to why things have not gone as easily as they would have liked.

Go back to your list of people and from the traits you have been taught, identify each individual by the characteristics they commonly display when you are dealing with them. Think about a consistent conversation you have with them when you just don't seem to break through to them on the issue.

The big question is are you defaulting to your natural style and speaking to them the way you are likely to listen or are you talking to them in style where they are likely to be receptive? Revisit those conversations in your head and try to see it from their point of view and how they are more likely to listen to what it is you are trying to get them to understand.

Ask yourself, do they have all the information they need? THINKER

Are you being to colorful and not just getting to the point and moving on? TELLER

Are you coming at them without developing some kind of rapport? TALKER

Are you giving them task to complete and a time frame and offering any help for them to accomplish these tasks? TASKER

Now that you are aware and starting to be equipped with the right perspective, what could you do differently to address these individuals going forward? If you are not sure of the persons EQ type, there are plenty of ways, tools and information you can draw upon to make that determination. In my book I have dedicated an entire chapter to the ways to identify and feel confident with your appraisal of their EQ.

Let's now think about the people you identified and assess their natural EQ and start to strategize how we might address them differently going forward.

Personal

1

2

3

4

5

Business

1

2

3

4

5

The Best Sales Professionals Are TRANSFORMERS

- They are perceptive and can emulate the personality trait they are interacting with.

- They have an EQ (Emotional Quotient) higher than most and can suppress their own natural tendencies of operating.

- This takes a keen sense of their own preferential trait and can modify their approach to be in the most appreciated way that their client finds it easy to listen.

THEY ARE THE BEST AT TALKING IN A WAY WHICH OTHERS ARE WILLING TO LISTEN

This is probably the most important statement I will make in this chapter. People will only listen in the way that is comfortable for them. Knowing how people are willing to listen is the key to being a great sales professional.

Once you have mastered both the ability to assess your client's personality traits and assimilate their communication style, your impact on the relationship will become a true, mutually beneficial and long-lasting one. This is what really differentiates the great sales people from the fantastic professional ones. Without a doubt, there are several studies on how to relate to other people, but then, one of the most effective ways to doing this is to mirror what the person in front of you is projecting.

THE SCIENCE OF THE SALE

There are many people who would argue that selling is not a science and yet I see new computer applications all the time that try to manage the selling process. There are things in science called Laws of Nature. Things like gravity, E=MC2 or the speed of light but there is one that people fail to recognize which is the 80/20 Principle that was suggested back in the late 1800's by Pareto, an Italian economists. He saw that 80 per cent of the world's wealth was controlled by 20 % of the population. Other scholars took that same principle and applied it to the work place and found that 80% or your results came from 20% of your efforts. This made a huge impact into the redevelopment of the world's economy after WWII.

Our modern day computers software and operating systems also were improved dramatically by Gates and Jobs. What they understood is that only 20% of the code written was used 80% of the time and they made that 20% easier to use and driven by icons and single strokes to lead to the PC.

In the business world if you were to take a close look at any company, you would find that 80% of your profits come from 20% of your product line. Also 80% of your sales come from 20% of your sales people and 80% of your business comes from 20% of your client base. Like any other law of nature if you try to oppose it in the long run you are going to lose. Knowing this it is time to put the principle to work for us in such a way that we can capitalize on it and exponentially improve our business.

So when it comes to your business, what's your 80/20 look like?

What are the 20% of your efforts you put out to get 80% of your results?

What are the products that you offer of which 20% accounts for 80% of your sales?

Of the people you deal with, who are the 20% that account for 80% of your sales?

Who are the 20% of your clients that promote 80% of your referrals?

In every business you need to understand the factors which truly drive your business. In my business there were three factors that I constantly monitored to make certain I was spending the appropriate amount of time with the clients that were truly supporting my business. I would consider the amount of total sales, the number of sales when they used me and the number of people they were willing to refer me to. So when I was about to leave for a week in my territory, I would have a list of these three categories and make certain my scheduler made appointments with the people on this list.

The first person contacted in each location was the number one seller of my offerings. They would have first crack with me to have a meeting in or out of the office. That might include meeting with them and one of their clients, participating in a seminar, going out to lunch or dinner with them and their spouse or business partner or maybe even a round of golf if they were so inclined. The next people I would visit are the people in the same office and try to see how I could help them grow their business with me or just to help them increase their overall business. Sometimes you have to help people with their business even though you might not benefit directly because if they are the right people will use you when they can when the next opportunity presents itself. Next people I would visit with are any people in the office that my best clients would refer me to or better yet introduce me too personally. This is one of the most important steps you should take if you are going to grow your business for the future. Referrals is the life blood of any business and if you don't take steps to cultivate them then you are left with cold calling for new business which is the hardest way to build a business.

So What Are Your Three Factors To Growing Your Business??

1.

2.

3.

It is very important the factors you chose are able to be measured easily and have significance in your business. So what does that mean? Look at your current business and see what you have some reporting on that you can begin to track. Maybe it is the volume of business total, maybe business in a certain product, maybe average sale size, maybe number of deals done or maybe it's the number of referrals they bring to the table whatever they are make certain they will help you monitor your business going forward.

Once you have completed this exercise now it is time to do the planning necessary to grow your business exponentially. You see once you have these key things in mind you can now start to really work the system to your benefit. By spending 80% of your time with the 20% that drive your business and deliver 80% of your results, life gets much easier and more control is in your corner. Working harder is never the answer but working smarter nets huge returns. If you work the system as I have explained it will work for you like it has for so many before.

One of the best ways to increase your business is through referrals and referrals lead to the best new clients. Once clients know you and like the attention they are getting, they are more than willing to offer you as a referral. The success of a referral is based on the depth of the introduction. If they offer you a referral as a passing comment that is not really a referral. If you are at an event or

in the same office, the best way to get a referral is to have the person walk you over and make the introduction. If that is not possible, you may ask them if they could call the individual while you are there and have them say you are a great partner in their business and they should definitely see or talk to you the next time you call. It is then imperative that you make the connection as quickly as possible.

This may seem uncomfortable at first but once you get in the habit your clients are more than happy to refer you to others. Also it is the perfect time for you to offer a referral to them. Ask them if there is anyone they have been trying to connect with and see if you can help them make that connection.

EXCERCISE

List 25 people you would like to be referred to. Look through your LINKEDIN contacts and see who your contacts know and who they might introduce too. There are always people that know other people you would like to know. Try connecting with them on your own and if they respond make certain that you thank them for connecting with you and use that as an opportunity to open a personal relationship.

Spend 80% of your time with the 20% of the people that deliver you more than 80% of your business. If there is anything you can shed to give you more time in front of your clients. There are probably things that you do you can hand off to someone more capable and can do the work done better, faster and cheaper. Remember we have done the exercise that shows you how valuable your time is.

So what are you going to do with the time freed up? Connect with people who can help you and who you can help. It is often easier to help others and has the possibility to produce more results.

The biggest question to ask yourself is are you ready and capable of change?

For years I have heard people talk about the ideas that it only takes 30 days to create a new habit. What they don't tell you is that it takes at least 9 months to stop an old one and the younger you learned and acquired it the longer it takes to change.

Recently I saw a video on YOUTUBE that showed an individual with a bike that was engineered so when you turned to the left it would go right and when you turned right it would go left. It took him nearly 9 months to recondition his thinking to be able to ride the bike. His 6 year old son who had just learned how to ride a bike was able to master it just within a few days. Why, because when we learn things we set up neurological pathways in our brains much like circuitry in a computer. In order to stop our brain from doing something we have ingrained in our minds it takes a conscious effort to break those old circuits and replace them with new wiring.

The reason I tell this story is because when you are used to doing things a certain way, it is much harder to break those habits than to establish new ones. In that effort you may find yourself frustrated and slipping back into old habits. This problem exists for everyone, no matter the level of your achievement. Pro athletes very often will employ a coach to help them achieve new skills because left to their own devices they are subject to slipping back into the comfortable ways they have mastered.

Taking the sports analogy further, many absolutely exceptional athletes will have many people helping them continue to hone and expand their skills. Football players will have a strength coach, speed coach, position coach, a nutritionists, a personal assistant, money manager and a sports phycologists. The whole reason is so they can continue to improve their craft and skills while others more capable and focused can manage their other affairs and hold them accountable.

So who is going to help you, be your coach, bring their expertise to the table and help you focus on what it is that will bring you to the next level and the next level after that. Might I suggest that our program has helped literally thousands of individuals bring their business to next level and we can do the same for you?

Check out the website www.selling8020.com and see some of the ways we can help. They include keynote speaking, seminar breakouts, workshops, webinars, blogs, videos and audios to keep you moving along a path of discovery and new possibilities.

www.ingramcontent.com/pod-product-compliance
Lightning Source LLC
Chambersburg PA
CBHW080532190526
45169CB00008B/3127